We Can Be Responsible!

WE TAKE CARE OF PETS

By Lynda Arnéz

Gareth Stevens
PUBLISHING

Please visit our website, www.garethstevens.com. For a free color catalog of all our high-quality books, call toll free 1-800-542-2595 or fax 1-877-542-2596.

Library of Congress Cataloging-in-Publication Data

Names: Arnéz, Lynda, author.
Title: We take care of pets / Lynda Arnez.
Description: New York : Gareth Stevens Publishing, [2020] | Series: We can be responsible! | Includes index.
Identifiers: LCCN 2018038705| ISBN 9781538239308 (paperback) | ISBN 9781538239322 (library bound) | ISBN 9781538239315 (6 pack)
Subjects: LCSH: Pets–Juvenile literature.
Classification: LCC SF413 .A76 2020 | DDC 636.088/7–dc23
LC record available at https://lccn.loc.gov/2018038705

First Edition

Published in 2020 by
Gareth Stevens Publishing
111 East 14th Street, Suite 349
New York, NY 10003

Editor: Kristen Nelson
Designer: Sarah Liddell

Photo credits: Cover, p. 1 Monkey Business Images/Shutterstock.com; p. 5 A3pfamily/Shutterstock.com; p. 7 ANURAK PONGPATIMET/Shutterstock.com; p. 9 Koltsov/Shutterstock.com; p. 11 Dusan Petkovic/Shutterstock.com; p. 13 eanstudio/Shutterstock.com; p. 15 Gemenacom/Shutterstock.com; pp. 17, 24 (fur) Lapina/Shutterstock.com; pp. 19, 24 (hutch) Lefebvre Alain/Shutterstock.com; p. 21 Santhosh Varghese/Shutterstock.com; p. 23 Helen Sushitskaya/Shutterstock.com.

Printed in the United States of America

CPSIA compliance information: Batch #CS19GS: For further information contact Gareth Stevens, New York, New York at 1-800-542-2595.

Contents

Pets are fun!
They need us to care
for them.

All pets need food!
Tai feeds his dog in a dish.

Will and Fred feed their bunny a carrot.

Donald feeds the fish.

Pets need exercise.
Hannah walks her dog.

Our hamster likes to run.
He runs in a wheel.

Pets need to be clean. Noreen brushes her cat's fur.

I clean the bunny house.
It is called a hutch.

We care for pets by showing them love! Chrissy kisses her bird's head.

How do you take care of your pet?

Words to Know

fur

hutch

Index